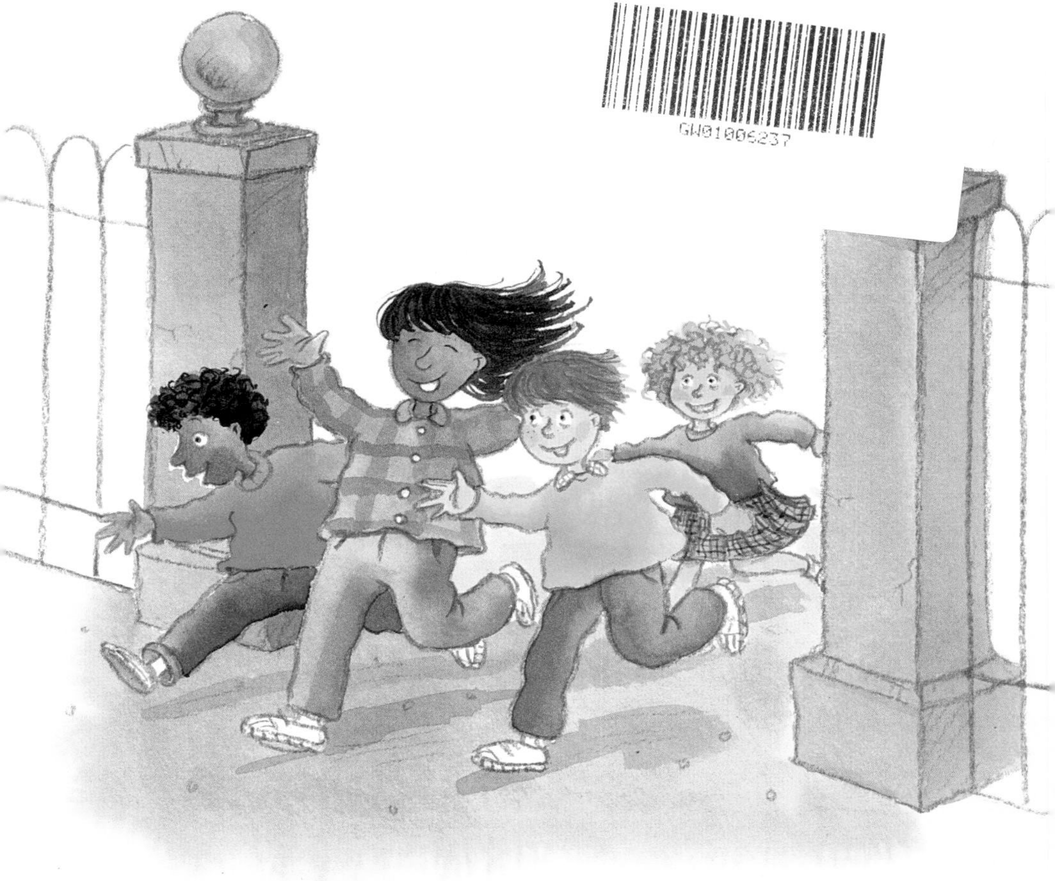

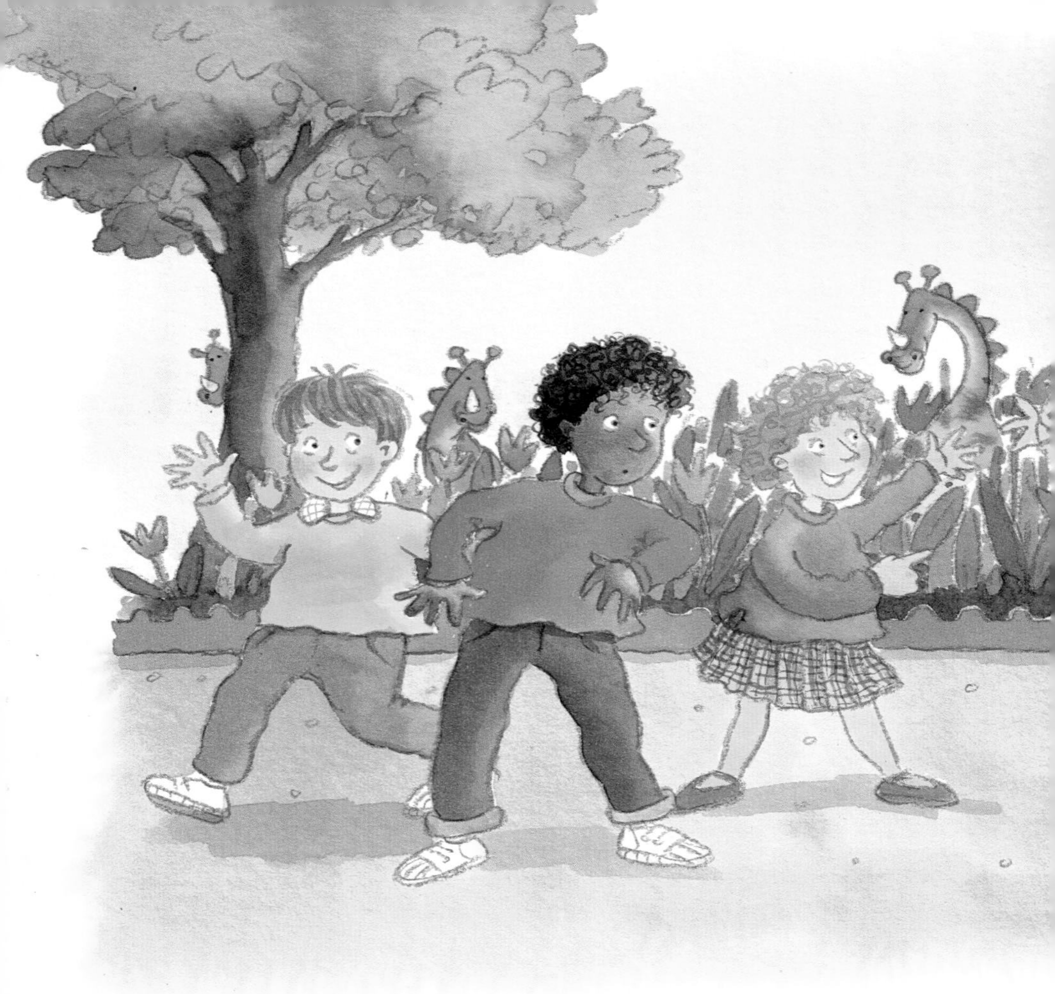

What shall we do today?

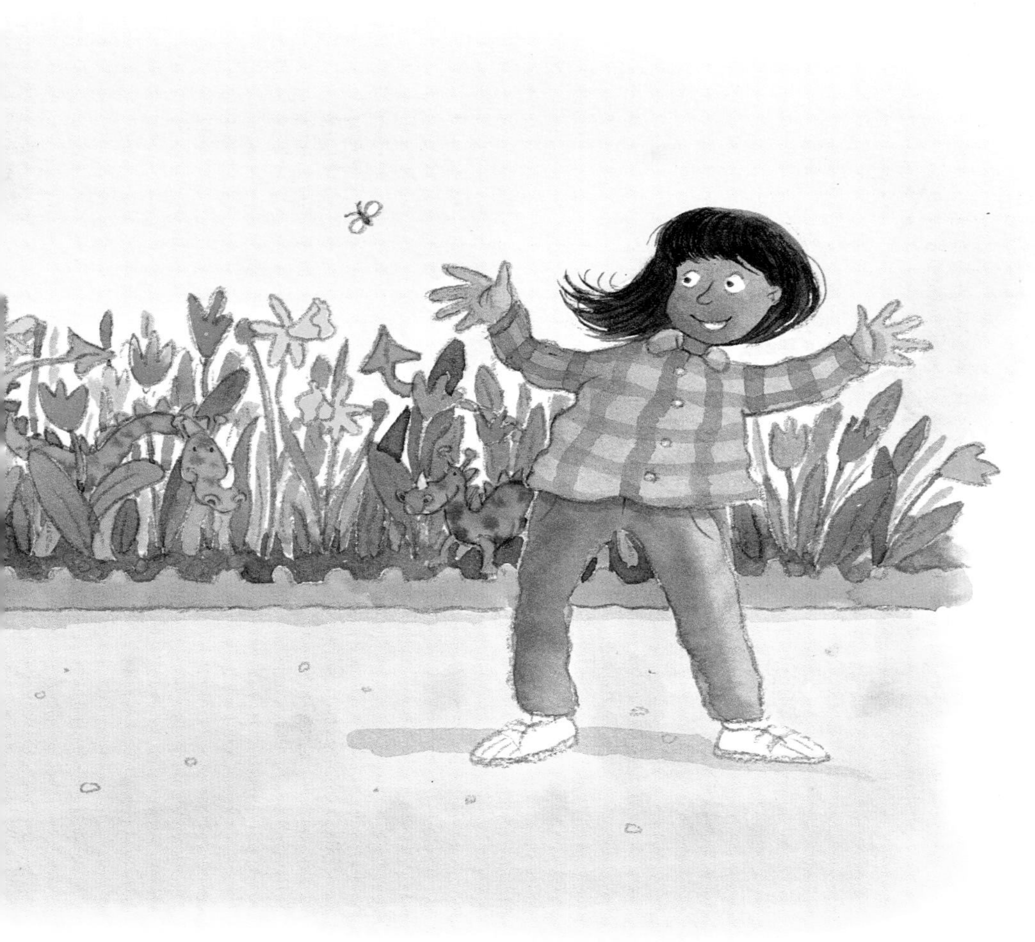

Look for dragons!

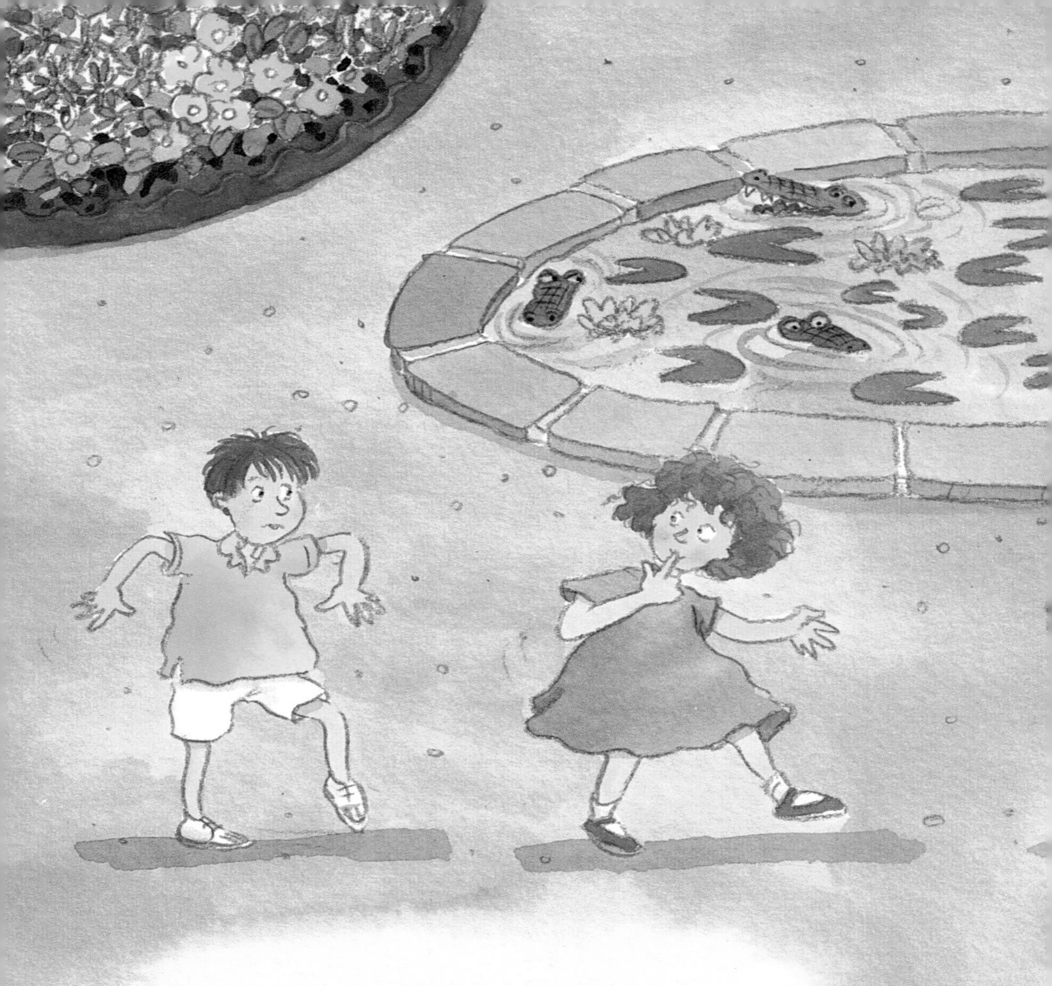

What shall we do today?

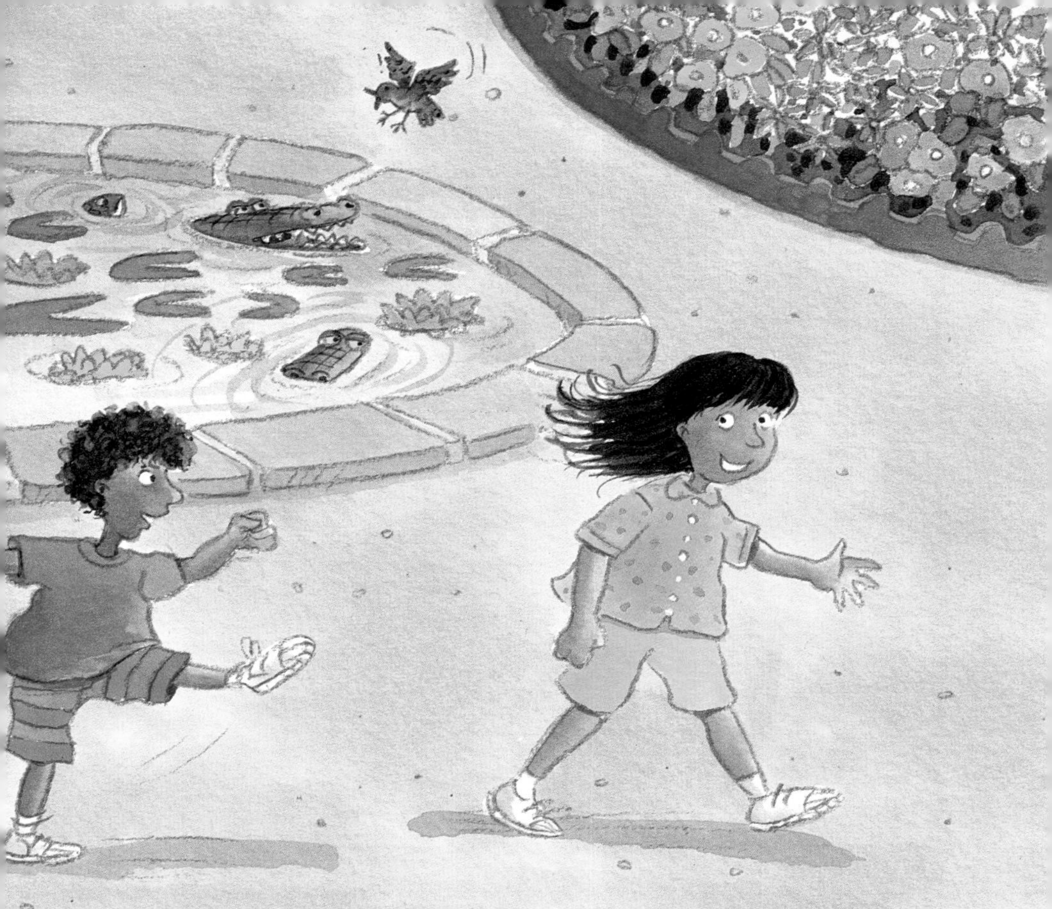

Look for crocodiles!

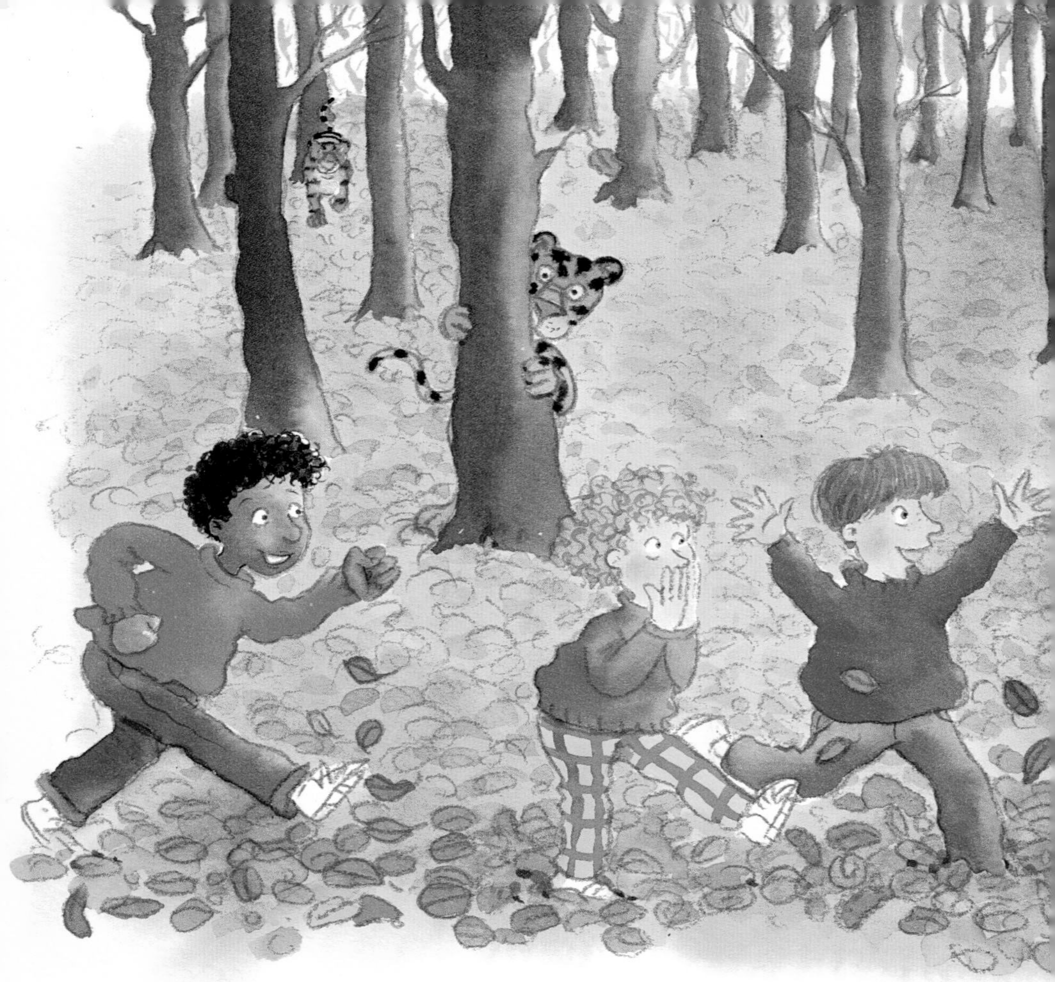

What shall we do today?

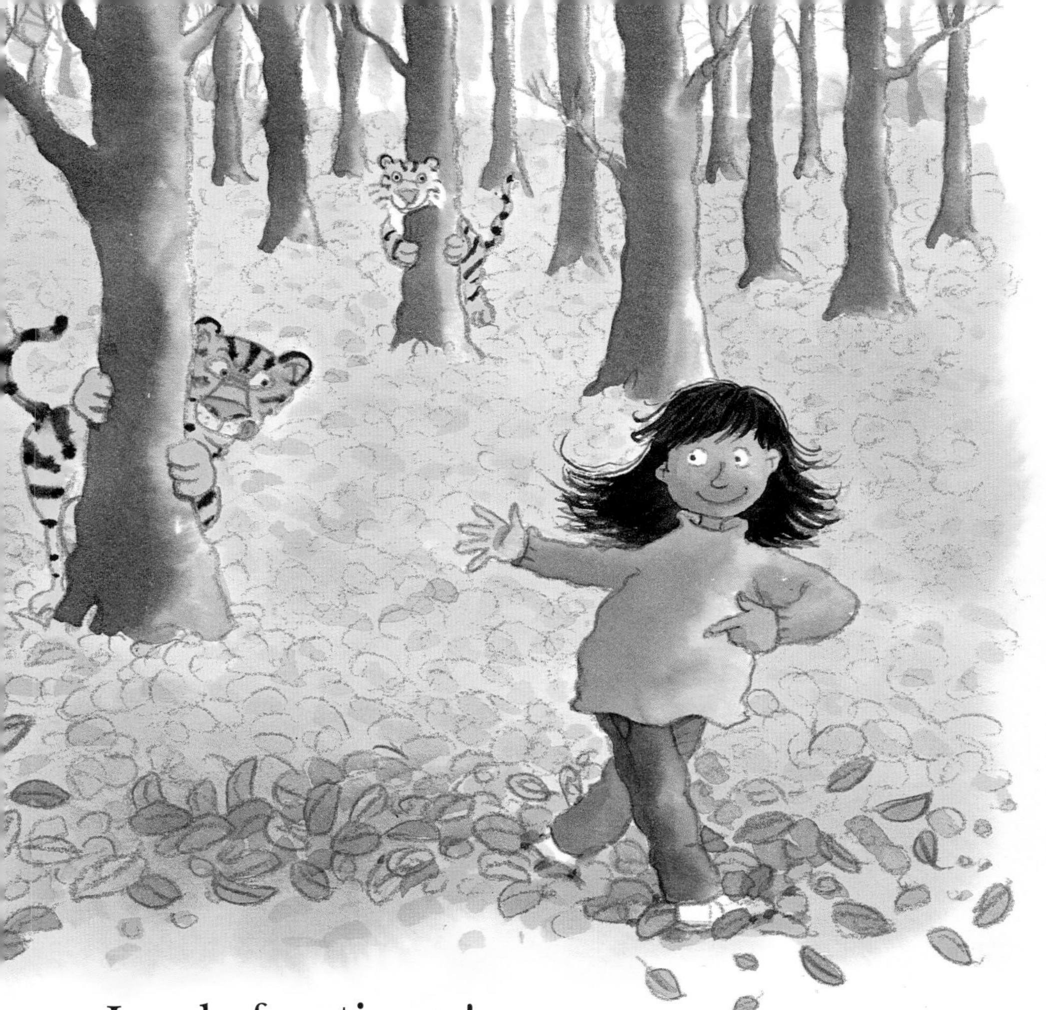

Look for tigers!

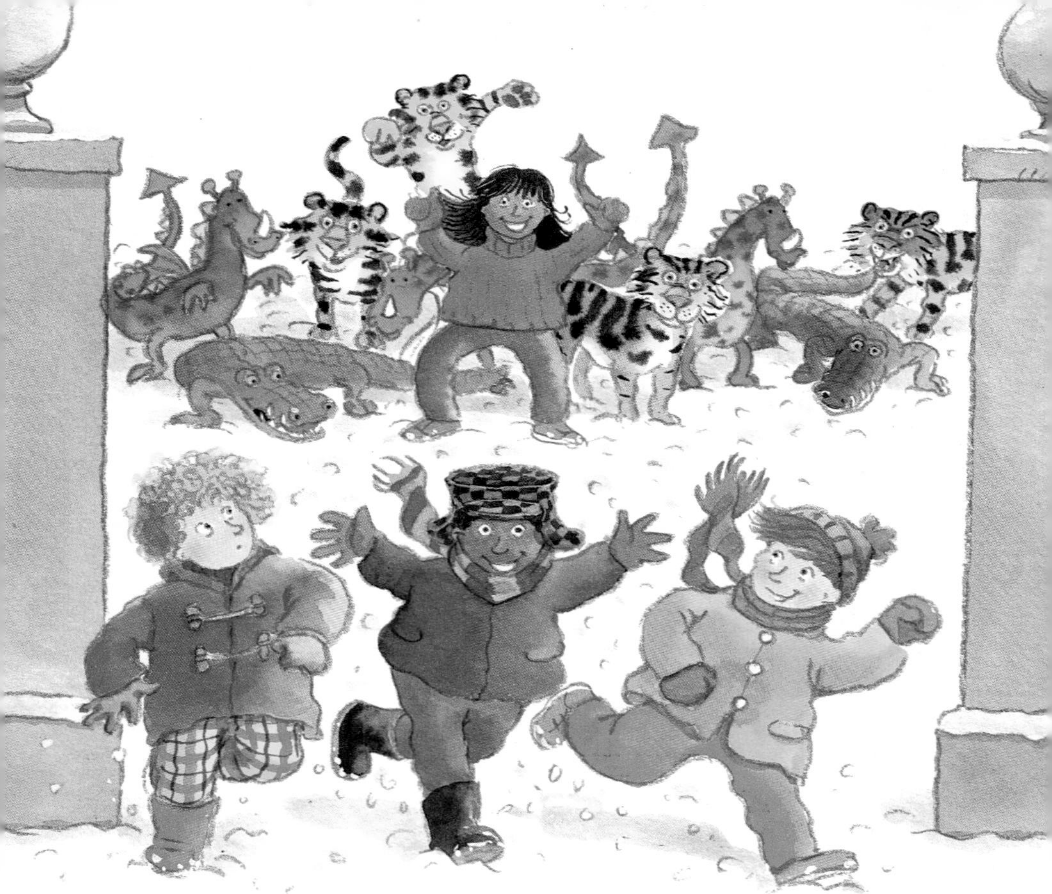

What shall we do today?
Run away!